Level 2 - ❶

W0099657

The Ottomans and Their Empire

Michael Wilkins

Series Editor **Rob Waring**

Level 2 - ❶

The Ottomans and Their Empire

Michael Wilkins

© 2017 Seed Learning, Inc.

Series Editor: Rob Waring
Acquisitions Editor: Liana Robinson
Copy Editor: Casey Malarcher
Cover/Interior Design: Andy Roh

ISBN: 978-1-9464-5206-1

10 9 8 7 6 5 4 3 2 1
21 20 19 18 17

Contents

Introduction ···················· 4

The Start of an Empire ········· 5

Sultans ························· 6

Constantinople ················· 7

Mehmed II ····················· 8

Christianity and Islam ·········· 9

Soldiers and Slaves ············ 10

Art and Design ················· 11

Business and Money ············ 12

Wars in the South and East ····· 13

Suleiman the Magnificent ······· 14

War in Europe ················· 15

The End of the Empire ·········· 16

Today ························· 17

Comprehension Questions ······· 18

Glossary ······················ 19

World History Timeline ········· 21

Introduction

The Ottomans were a family from a small town in Turkey long ago. They became one of the most important families in history. This is the story of how one family made a big empire that lasted about 600 years.

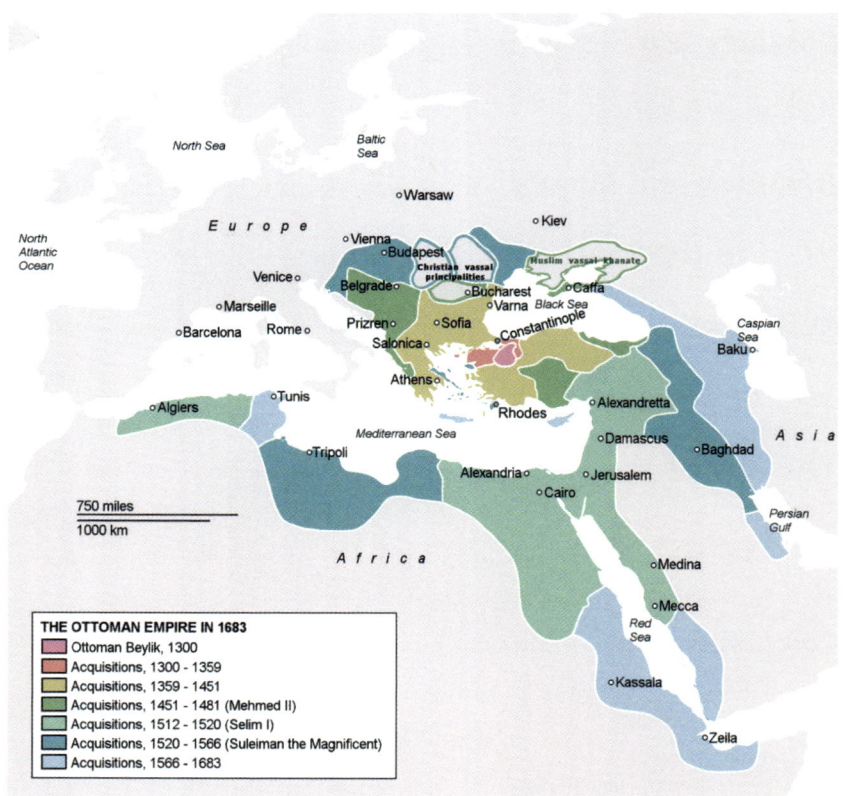

THE OTTOMAN EMPIRE IN 1683
- Ottoman Beylik, 1300
- Acquisitions, 1300 - 1359
- Acquisitions, 1359 - 1451
- Acquisitions, 1451 - 1481 (Mehmed II)
- Acquisitions, 1512 - 1520 (Selim I)
- Acquisitions, 1520 - 1566 (Suleiman the Magnificent)
- Acquisitions, 1566 - 1683

The Start of an Empire

A man called Osman I started the empire. He was the leader of a small town called Sogut. He had big ideas for the future.

One day, Osman had a dream that he would make a great empire and become a powerful leader. In time, Osman's dream came true as he and his family used their power to take over many cities and towns.

Osman I

Sultans

The leader of the Ottoman Empire was called a Sultan. The Sultan had a lot of power, like a king. Osman was the first Sultan.

Sultan Bayezid I
(1389 - 1402)

After Osman died, a new sultan took his place. Then another sultan came after that. Each new sultan used his fast horses to take more towns, and the empire continued to grow.

Sultan Mehmed I
(1413 - 1421)

Sultan Selim III
1789 - 1807

6

Constantinople

Long ago, the city of Istanbul was called Constantinople. It was one of the greatest cities in the old world. Hagia Sophia was its greatest church. The Ottomans wanted Constantinople. They wanted to make it their home.

Inside Hagia Sophia

A Christian picture in Hagia Sophia

Hagia Sophia

Mehmed II

The seventh sultan after Osman was named Mehmed II (1444 - 1446, 1451 - 1481). He decided to take Constantinople. First, he stopped ships from going in

A cannon

or out of the city. Then he attacked. He used a new weapon called a cannon which broke down the city walls. He used many soldiers to finally take the city. The battle took many days.

Sultan Mehmed II entering Constantinople

An Ottoman soldier on a horse

8

Christianity and Islam

Old Constantinople was Christian, but the Ottomans were Muslim. The Ottomans changed many things. They changed the biggest church called the Hagia Sophia into a mosque, which it still is today. The Blue Mosque was also built by the Ottomans. It is one of the most beautiful mosques ever built.

The Blue Mosque from the water

Inside the Blue Mosque

The Blue Mosque at night

Soldiers and Slaves

The Ottomans were Muslims, but non-Muslims could stay in the empire. However, there was a tax for non-Muslims. Some children (mostly Christian boys) were taken from their families as a tax. The smartest were sent to special schools. The others were trained to be soldiers. All of them had to follow Islam.

An Ottoman soldier

Inside Topkapi Palace

Topkapi Palace—where the sultan lived and where children were taught

Art and Design

Many of the Ottomans loved art. Constantinople became home to artists from all over the empire. These artists made Constantinople into the most beautiful city in the world. Ottoman art is famous for its detailed designs. The designs can be seen on many things. Especially, on the walls of mosques.

Wall design

A beautifully decorated hall

Plate design

Hand-painted wall tiles, Topkapi Palace

Business and Money

How did the Ottomans pay for everything? The Ottoman Empire was between Europe and Asia. They made a lot of money by buying and selling things to the east and west. The Ottomans became rich.

Spices

Gold and jewels

Rugs and cloth

Wars in the South and East

The Hadj in Mecca

But the Ottomans were not satisfied. They wanted more land. In time, they took Egypt, Iran, and Arabia. They controlled most of the Muslim countries in the world and important Muslim cities, like Mecca in Arabia.

The Sphinx and Pyramids in Egypt

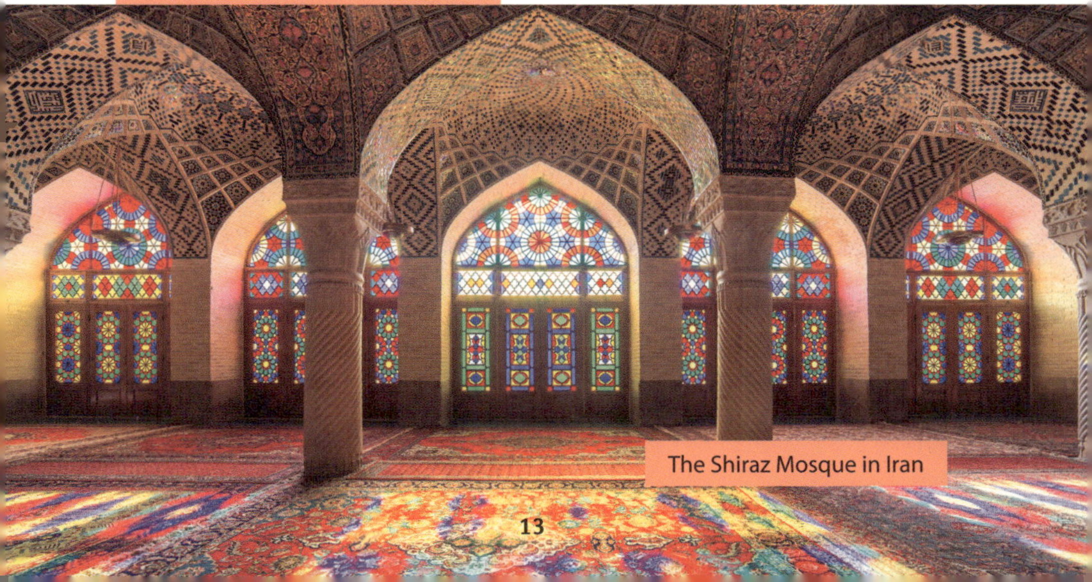

They felt strong and rich. They were ready to fight Europe.

The Shiraz Mosque in Iran

Suleiman the Magnificent

Suleiman (1520 - 1566) was the greatest of all the Ottoman Sultans. He was the leader of the Muslim world. Constantinople was the

Sultan Suleiman

greatest city in the world, but he wanted more land, so he attacked Europe and Asia.

Ottoman soldiers on horseback

Suleymaniye Mosque

War in Europe

Suleiman and the Ottomans won many battles against the Europeans. They took a lot of territory in Europe. Christians in Europe were very afraid of the Ottomans. Parents told children that if they were not quiet, an Ottoman would get them.

The siege of Malta

The Ottomans even attacked Vienna in the middle of Europe, but the European armies stopped them.

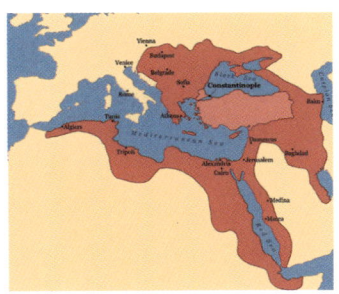

The Ottoman Empire in 1683

The End of the Empire

The Ottoman Empire fought on the losing side in World War I. By October of 1918, the Ottomans were out of the war. During peace talks, the empire was divide up. In 1923, the Republic of Turkey was born.

President Ataturk
(the first president of
Turkey from 1923-1938)

Flag of Turkey

Monument of the Republic, Taksim Square

Today

The Republic of Turkey is an interesting country. Every year, many tourists visit to enjoy its beaches, art, food, and historical sites.

Turkish food

In fact, we can still see many things from the time of the Ottoman Empire. If you go to Istanbul—which used to be Constantinople—you can see many of the Ottoman buildings talked about in this book.

Turkish people showing national pride

Turkish tea

Comprehension Questions

1. Where were the Ottomans from?
   - (a) Constantinople
   - (b) Vienna
   - (c) Sogut
   - (d) Istanbul

2. What was the Ottoman king called?
   - (a) King
   - (b) Prince
   - (c) President
   - (d) Sultan

3. What is the city of Constantinople called now?
   - (a) Cairo
   - (b) Rome
   - (c) Vienna
   - (d) Istanbul

4. What religion did the Ottomans follow?
   - (a) Islam
   - (b) Buddhism
   - (c) Christianity
   - (d) Hinduism

5. About how long did the Ottoman Empire last?
   - (a) 200 years
   - (b) 400 years
   - (c) 600 years
   - (d) 800 years

6. Which country did the Ottomans NOT control?
   - (a) Egypt
   - (b) Iran
   - (c) Austria
   - (d) Turkey

7. How did the Ottomans make their money?
   - (a) By printing it
   - (b) By trade
   - (c) By farming
   - (d) By stealing it

8. Who was the first sultan?
   - (a) Mehmed
   - (b) Ataturk
   - (c) Suleiman
   - (d) Osman

9. What is Hagia Sophia today?
   - (a) A church
   - (b) A mosque
   - (c) A theater
   - (d) A restaurant

10. When was the Ottoman Empire divided up?
    - (a) After World War I
    - (b) During World War II
    - (c) Before Egypt fell
    - (d) When Ataturk became president

Glossary

- **attack** to make a sudden, violent attempt to hurt or damage

- **battle** a big fight between two groups of soldiers

- **cannon** a very large gun

- **Christian** someone whose religion is Christianity

- **Christianity** a religion based on belief in one God and the teachings of Jesus Christ

- **empire** a group of countries ruled by one nation

- **Islam** a religion based on belief in one God and the teachings of Mohammed

- **magnificent** very good

- **mosque** a building used for a worship by Muslims

- **Muslim** someone whose religion is Islam

- **satisfied** happy; pleased

- **slave** a person who is owned by someone else

- **soldier** a fighter in an army

- **sultan** a king or ruler in some Muslim countries

- **tax** money, goods, or services that must be paid to a government

Image Credit/Pages

World History
Timeline

This chart shows a rough overview of world history.
Some of the dates have been simplified.

World History Timeline

2900 BC	2800 BC	2700 BC	2600 BC	2500 BC

Narmer, Egyptian King
(c. 3000 BC)

Pyramids of Giza
(built c. 2550-2490 BC)

Cuneiform (c. 3000 BC-100 AD)

Old Egyptian Kingdom (c. 2686 BC)

2900 BC	2800 BC	2700 BC	2600 BC	2500 BC

◄ 5000 BC   Mesopotamia (Sumerians)

◄ 3100 BC   Early Dynastic Period of Egypt   Old Egyptian Kingdom

◄ 3650 BC   Minoan Civilization (Crete)

Early Bronze Age

2900 BC	2800 BC	2700 BC	2600 BC	2500 BC

World History Timeline

| 2400 BC | 2300 BC | 2200 BC | 2100 BC | 2000 BC |

Sahure, Egyptian King
(c. 2487-2475 BC)

Indus Valley
Civilization

Sargon the Great,
Akkadian King
(c. 2340-2284 BC)

Gudea of Lagash
(c. 2144-2124 BC)

Ur III Dynasty (c. 2112-2004 BC)

| 2400 BC | 2300 BC | 2200 BC | 2100 BC | 2000 BC |

Xia Dynasty

Gutian Dynasty

Elam (Iran)

Akkadian Empire

Ur III Dynasty

Assyria (Early Period)

Middle Egyptian Kingdom

Minoan Civilization (Crete)

1st Intermediate
Period

Indus Valley Civilization (India)

| 2400 BC | 2300 BC | 2200 BC | 2100 BC | 2000 BC |

World History Timeline

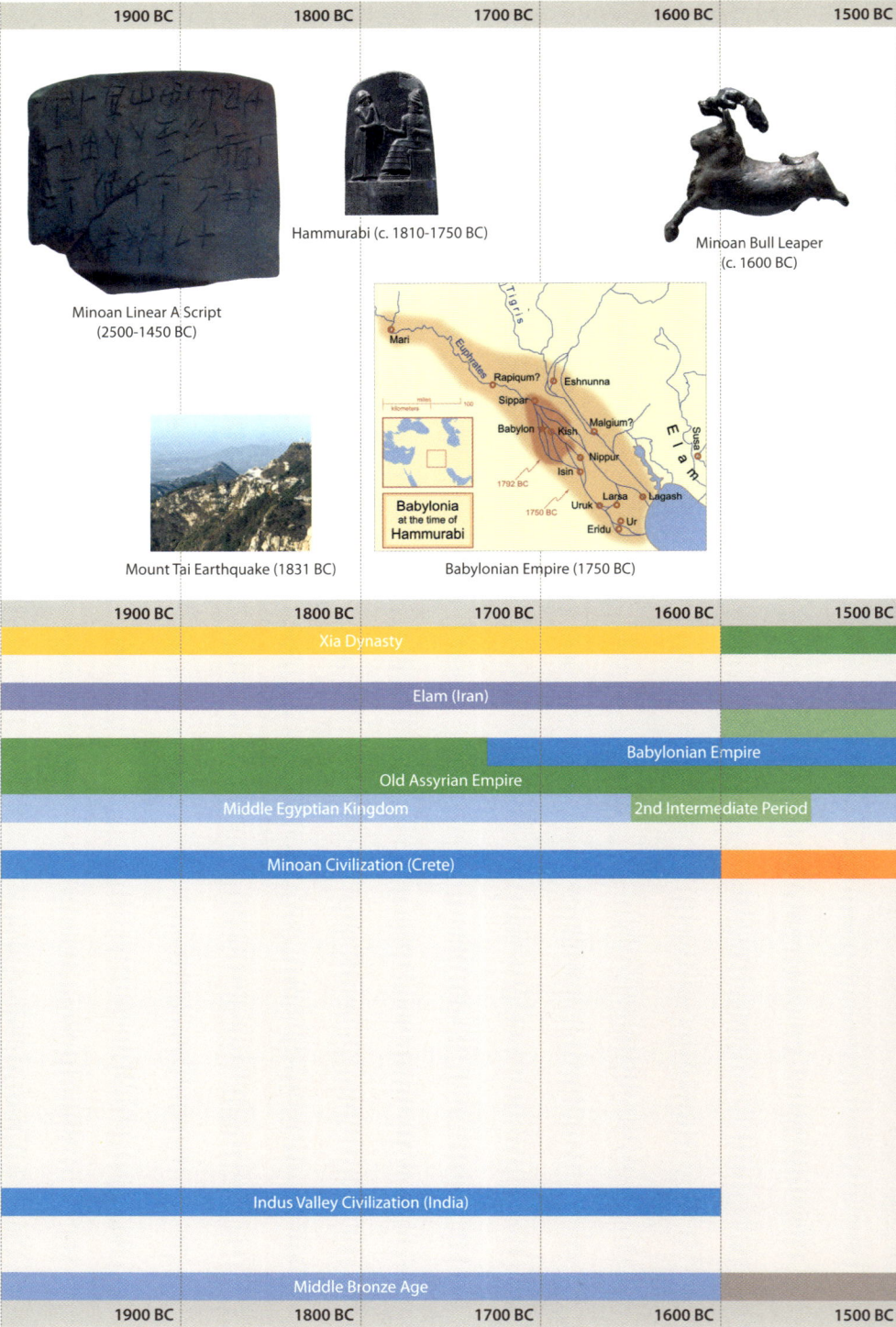

1900 BC	1800 BC	1700 BC	1600 BC	1500 BC

Minoan Linear A Script
(2500-1450 BC)

Hammurabi (c. 1810-1750 BC)

Minoan Bull Leaper
(c. 1600 BC)

Mount Tai Earthquake (1831 BC)

Babylonia at the time of Hammurabi

Babylonian Empire (1750 BC)

1900 BC	1800 BC	1700 BC	1600 BC	1500 BC

Xia Dynasty

Elam (Iran)

Babylonian Empire

Old Assyrian Empire

Middle Egyptian Kingdom

2nd Intermediate Period

Minoan Civilization (Crete)

Indus Valley Civilization (India)

Middle Bronze Age

1900 BC	1800 BC	1700 BC	1600 BC	1500 BC

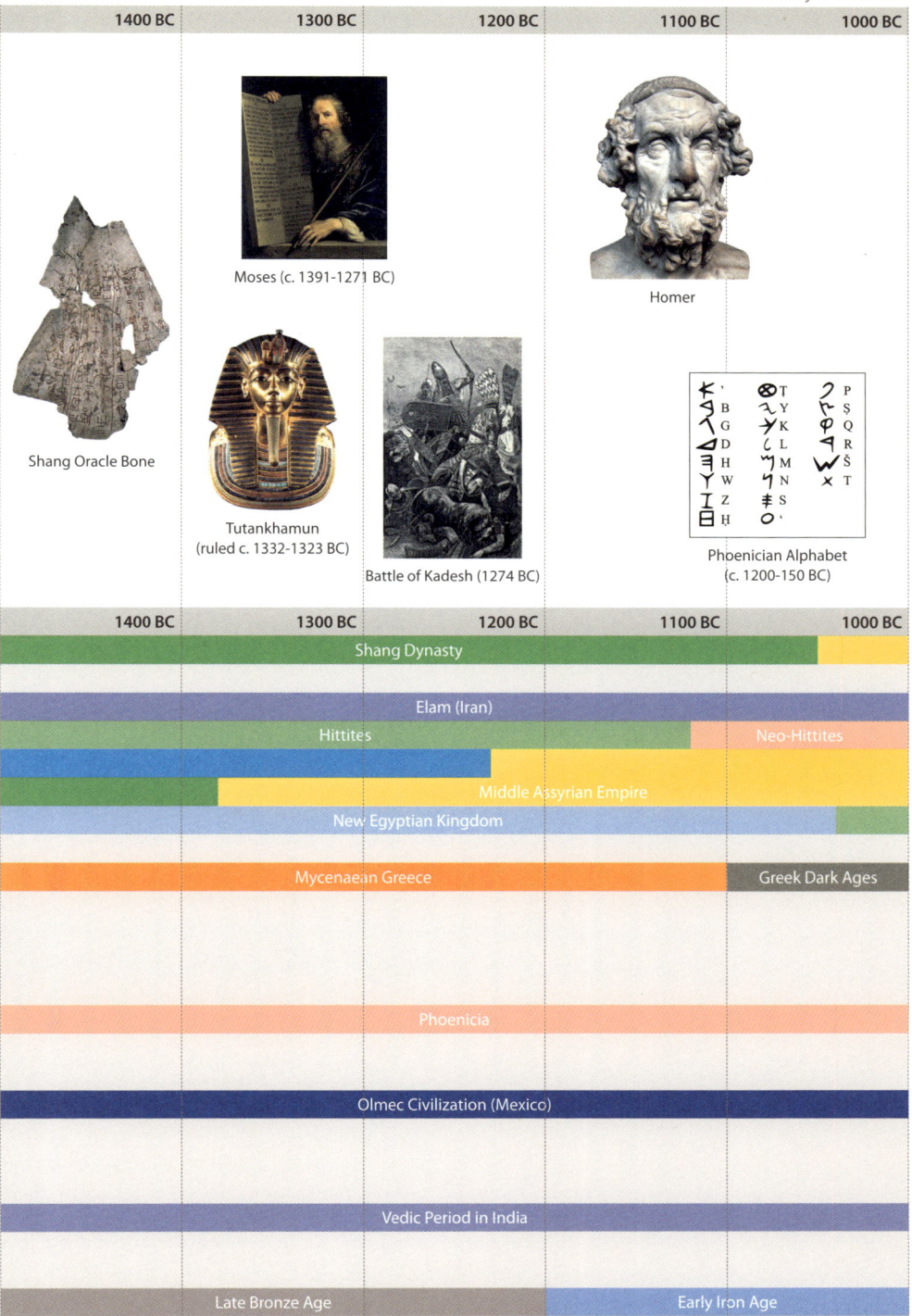

World History Timeline

1400 BC	1300 BC	1200 BC	1100 BC	1000 BC

Moses (c. 1391-1271 BC)

Homer

Shang Oracle Bone

Tutankhamun
(ruled c. 1332-1323 BC)

Battle of Kadesh (1274 BC)

Phoenician Alphabet
(c. 1200-150 BC)

1400 BC	1300 BC	1200 BC	1100 BC	1000 BC

Shang Dynasty

Elam (Iran)

Hittites

Neo-Hittites

Middle Assyrian Empire

New Egyptian Kingdom

Mycenaean Greece

Greek Dark Ages

Phoenicia

Olmec Civilization (Mexico)

Vedic Period in India

Late Bronze Age

Early Iron Age

1400 BC	1300 BC	1200 BC	1100 BC	1000 BC

World History Timeline

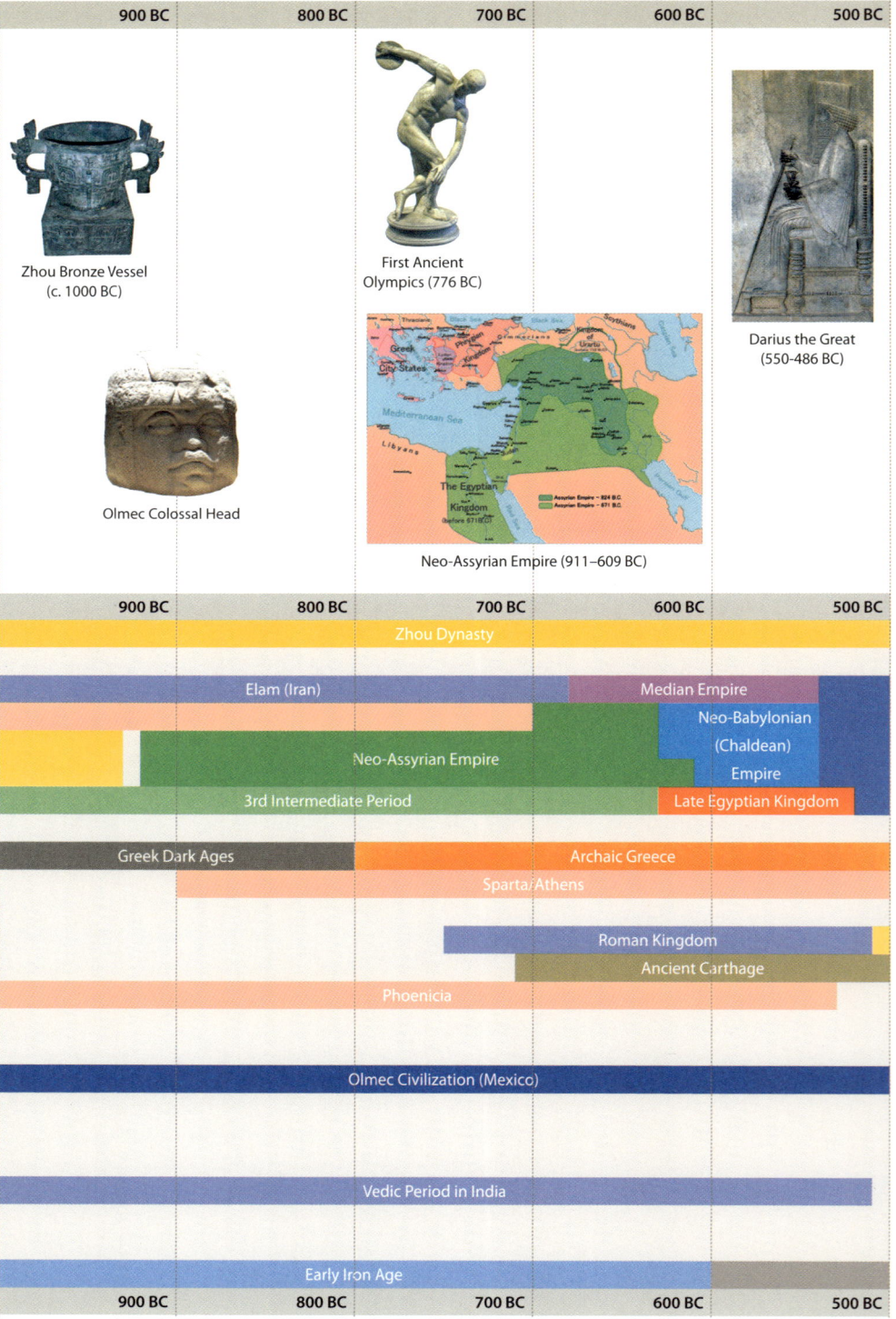

900 BC	800 BC	700 BC	600 BC	500 BC

Zhou Bronze Vessel
(c. 1000 BC)

First Ancient
Olympics (776 BC)

Darius the Great
(550-486 BC)

Olmec Colossal Head

Neo-Assyrian Empire (911–609 BC)

900 BC	800 BC	700 BC	600 BC	500 BC

Zhou Dynasty

Elam (Iran)

Median Empire

Neo-Babylonian (Chaldean) Empire

Neo-Assyrian Empire

3rd Intermediate Period

Late Egyptian Kingdom

Greek Dark Ages

Archaic Greece

Sparta/Athens

Roman Kingdom

Ancient Carthage

Phoenicia

Olmec Civilization (Mexico)

Vedic Period in India

Early Iron Age

900 BC	800 BC	700 BC	600 BC	500 BC

| 400 BC | 300 BC | 200 BC | 100 BC | 0 |

Alexander the Great
(356-323 BC)

Julius Caesar
(100-44 BC)

Hannibal
(247-183 BC)

Cleopatra
(69-30 BC)

Battle of Salamis
(480 BC)

Seleucid Empire (312-63 BC)

Rossetta Stone
(created 196 BC)

| 400 BC | 300 BC | 200 BC | 100 BC | 0 |

Zhou Dynasty · Qin · Han Dynasty

Achaemenid (Persian) Empire

Alexander the Great

Parthian Empire

Seleucid Empire
Ptolemaic Kingdom
(Hellenistic Greece)

Classical Greece

Sparta/Athens

Roman Empire

Roman Republic

Roman Empire

Maurya Empire

Middle Iron Age

| 400 BC | 300 BC | 200 BC | 100 BC | 0 |

World History Timeline

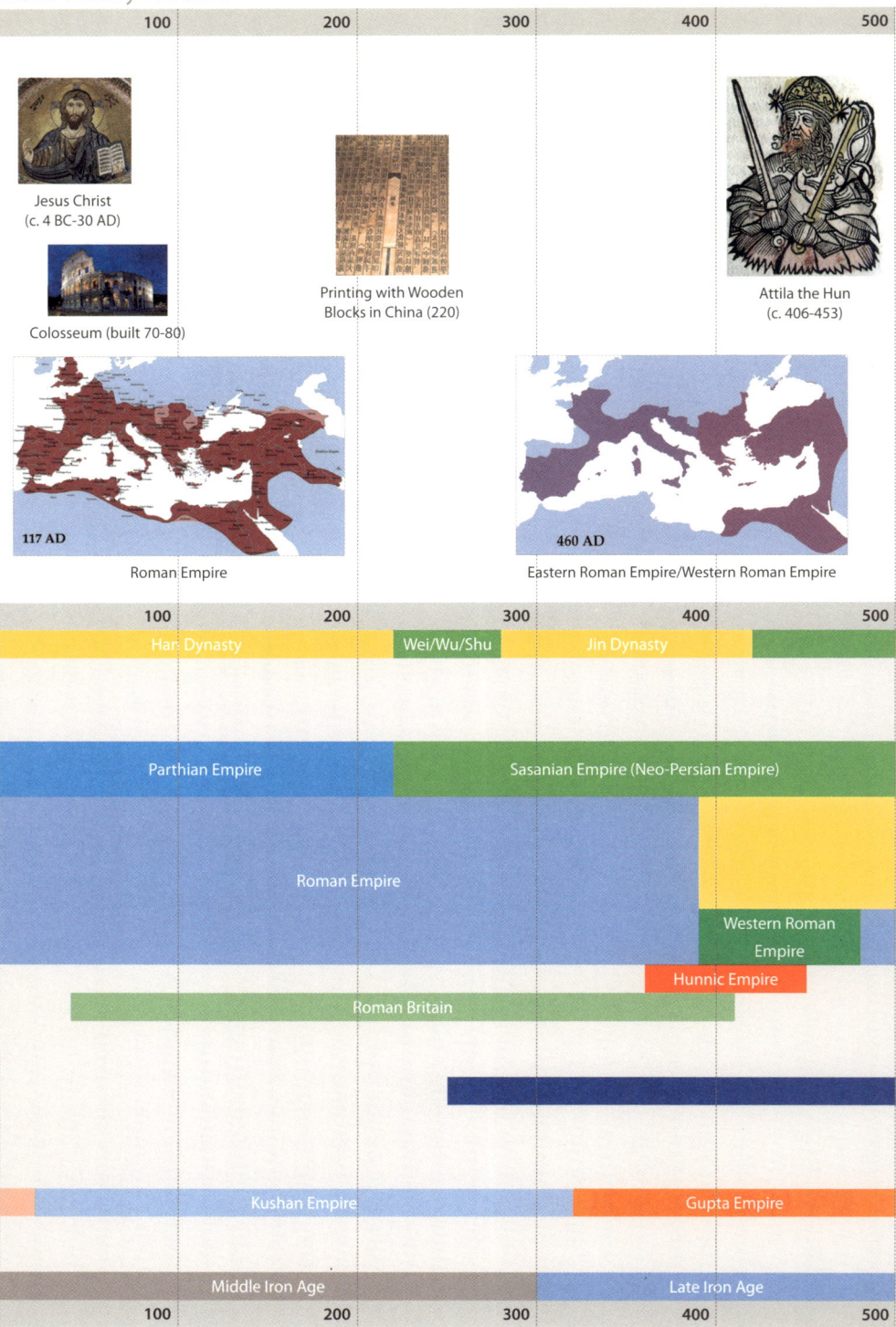

Jesus Christ
(c. 4 BC–30 AD)

Colosseum (built 70–80)

Printing with Wooden
Blocks in China (220)

Attila the Hun
(c. 406–453)

117 AD

460 AD

Roman Empire

Eastern Roman Empire/Western Roman Empire

100	200	300	400	500

Han Dynasty — Wei/Wu/Shu — Jin Dynasty

Parthian Empire — Sasanian Empire (Neo-Persian Empire)

Roman Empire

Western Roman Empire

Hunnic Empire

Roman Britain

Kushan Empire — Gupta Empire

Middle Iron Age — Late Iron Age

100	200	300	400	500

World History Timeline

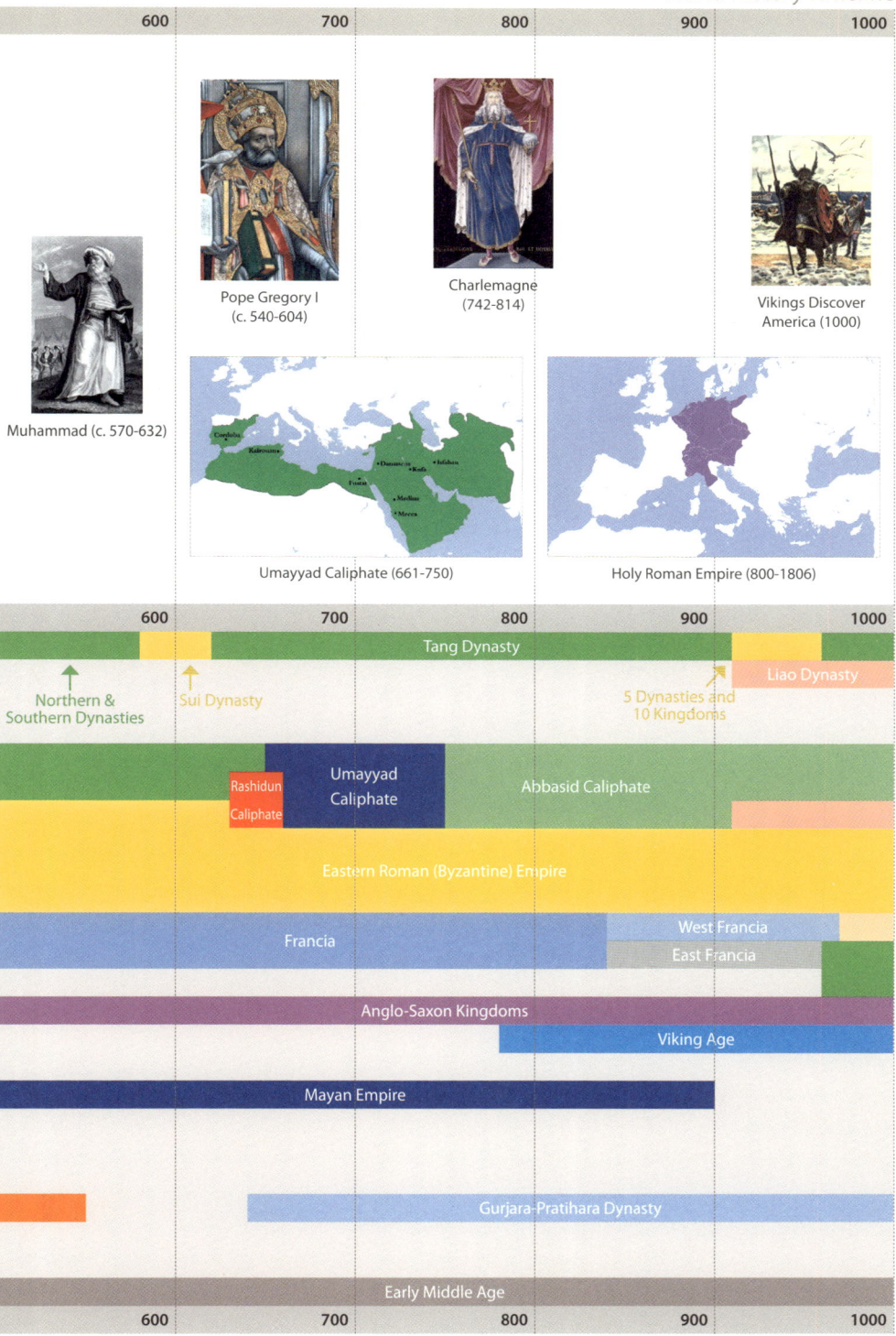

Muhammad (c. 570-632)

Pope Gregory I (c. 540-604)

Charlemagne (742-814)

Vikings Discover America (1000)

Umayyad Caliphate (661-750)

Holy Roman Empire (800-1806)

600 | 700 | 800 | 900 | 1000

Tang Dynasty

Liao Dynasty

Northern & Southern Dynasties

Sui Dynasty

5 Dynasties and 10 Kingdoms

Rashidun Caliphate

Umayyad Caliphate

Abbasid Caliphate

Eastern Roman (Byzantine) Empire

Francia

West Francia

East Francia

Anglo-Saxon Kingdoms

Viking Age

Mayan Empire

Gurjara-Pratihara Dynasty

Early Middle Age

600 | 700 | 800 | 900 | 1000

World History Timeline

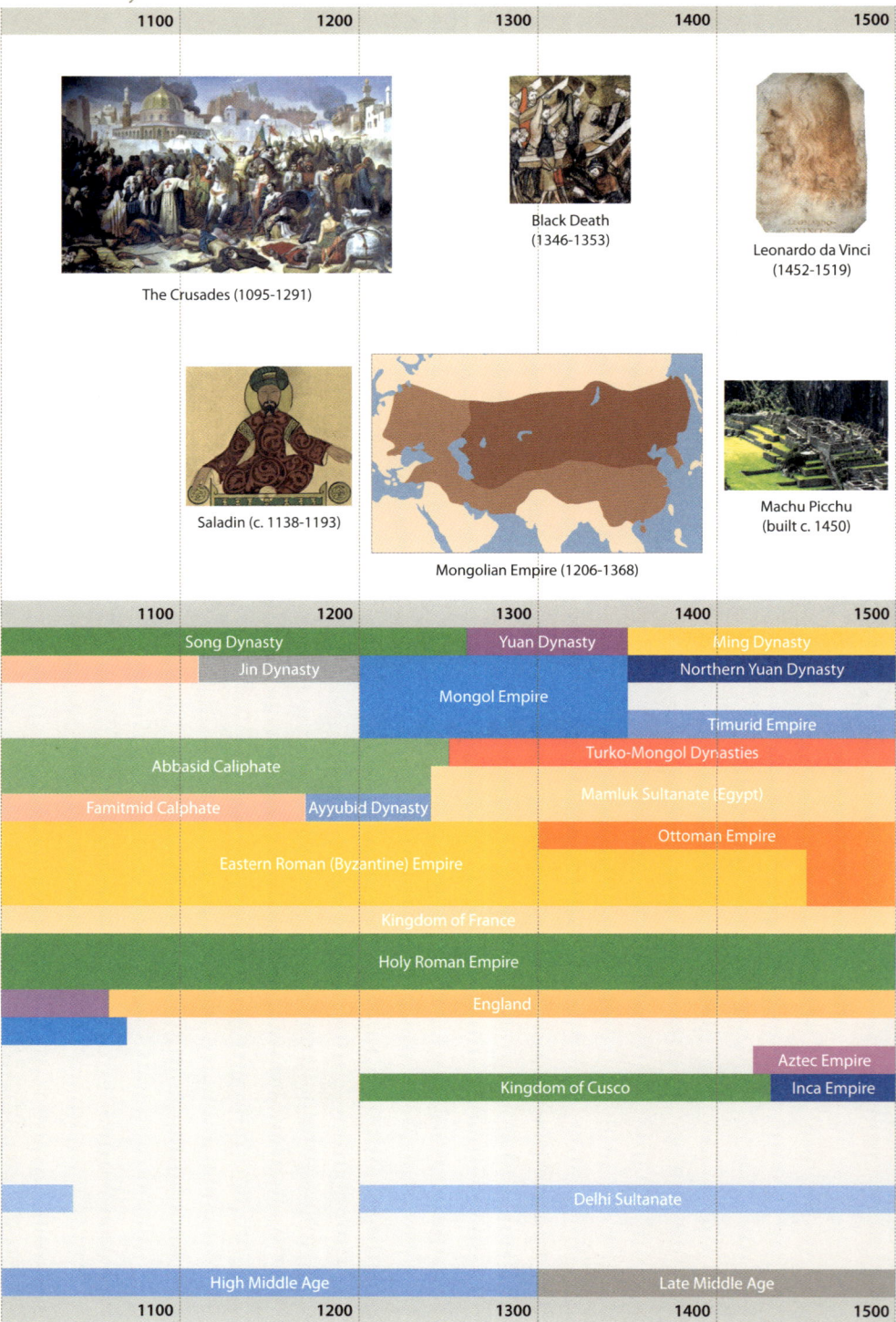

1100	1200	1300	1400	1500

The Crusades (1095-1291)

Black Death (1346-1353)

Leonardo da Vinci (1452-1519)

Saladin (c. 1138-1193)

Mongolian Empire (1206-1368)

Machu Picchu (built c. 1450)

1100	1200	1300	1400	1500

Song Dynasty

Yuan Dynasty

Ming Dynasty

Jin Dynasty

Northern Yuan Dynasty

Mongol Empire

Timurid Empire

Abbasid Caliphate

Turko-Mongol Dynasties

Famitmid Calphate

Ayyubid Dynasty

Mamluk Sultanate (Egypt)

Ottoman Empire

Eastern Roman (Byzantine) Empire

Kingdom of France

Holy Roman Empire

England

Aztec Empire

Kingdom of Cusco

Inca Empire

Delhi Sultanate

High Middle Age

Late Middle Age

1100	1200	1300	1400	1500

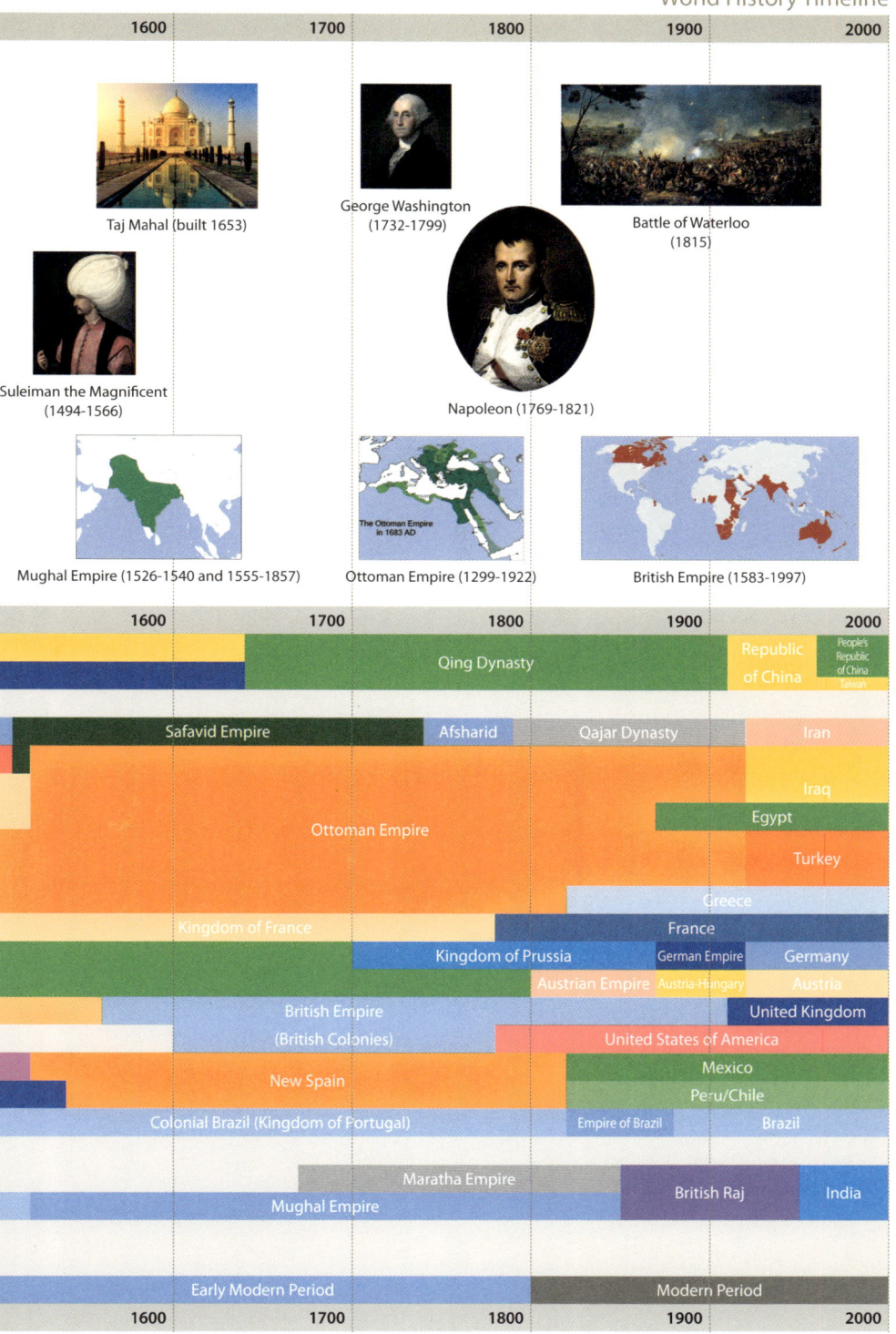

World History Timeline

| 1600 | 1700 | 1800 | 1900 | 2000 |

Taj Mahal (built 1653)

George Washington (1732-1799)

Battle of Waterloo (1815)

Suleiman the Magnificent (1494-1566)

Napoleon (1769-1821)

Mughal Empire (1526-1540 and 1555-1857)

The Ottoman Empire in 1683 AD

Ottoman Empire (1299-1922)

British Empire (1583-1997)

| 1600 | 1700 | 1800 | 1900 | 2000 |

Qing Dynasty

Republic of China

People's Republic of China
Taiwan

Safavid Empire

Afsharid

Qajar Dynasty

Iran

Iraq

Ottoman Empire

Egypt

Turkey

Greece

Kingdom of France

France

Kingdom of Prussia

German Empire

Germany

Austrian Empire

Austria-Hungary

Austria

British Empire (British Colonies)

United Kingdom

United States of America

New Spain

Mexico

Peru/Chile

Colonial Brazil (Kingdom of Portugal)

Empire of Brazil

Brazil

Maratha Empire

British Raj

India

Mughal Empire

Early Modern Period

Modern Period

| 1600 | 1700 | 1800 | 1900 | 2000 |

List of Books

LEVEL 1

1. Calendars and the History of Time
2. Searching for El Dorado
3. The Tower of Babel
4. The Pilgrim Fathers
5. Traveling on the Silk Road
6. The Invention of Writing
7. The Making of a United Europe
8. The Magic of Numbers
9. The Persian Empire
10. The Great Wall of China

LEVEL 2

1. The Ottomans and Their Empire
2. The War Between the States
3. The Industrial Revolution
4. The Agricultural Revolution
5. Wars in the Middle East
6. The British Empire, Then and Now
7. The Neo-Assyrian Empire
8. The Rise and Fall of Communism
9. The History of Printing
10. The Vikings and Erik the Red

LEVEL 3

1. Space Exploration
2. The Spanish Conquest of the Americas
3. Cleopatra
4. The French Revolution
5. Benjamin Franklin
6. Galileo Galilei
7. The Battle of Salamis
8. Tea and Wars
9. Christopher Columbus
10. The Trojan War

LEVEL 4

1. Alexander the Great
2. Leonardo da Vinci
3. The Neo-Babylonian Empire
4. The Birth of the United States of America
5. Life and Death in Ancient Egypt
6. Life in the Roman Army
7. The Great Plane Race
8. Genghis Khan
9. Korea: A Land Divided by War
10. The Crusades

LEVEL 5

1. The Story of the Renaissance
2. The Great Plague
3. The Mughal Empire
4. Popes and Kings in the Middle Ages
5. Tutankhamun
6. The Story of the Reformation
7. The Medical Revolution
8. Decisive Battles of World War II
9. China: The New Superpower
10. The Great Depression

LEVEL 6

1. World War I
2. Communication Technology
3. The First Democracies
4. The Cold War
5. Global Trade and Peace
6. Greek Culture
7. Napoleon
8. The History of Transportation
9. Capitalism: Good or Evil?
10. China's First Empire: The Qin Dynasty